Accès Studio

Michael Wardle

Heinemann is an imprint of Pearson Education Limited, a company incorporated in England and Wales, having its registered office at Edinburgh Gate, Harlow, Essex, CM20 2JE. Registered company number: 872828

www.pearsonschoolsandfecolleges.co.uk

Heinemann is a registered trademark of Pearson Education Limited

Text © Pearson Education Limited 2010

First published 2010

16
13

British Library Cataloguing in Publication Data
A catalogue record for this book is available from the British Library

ISBN 978 0 435 02722 3

Edited by Fabienne Tartarin
Designed by Emily Hunter-Higgins
Typeset by HL Studios, Long Hanborough, Oxford
Original illustrations © Pearson Education Limited 2010
Illustrated by Andrew Painter
Cover design by Emily Hunter-Higgins
Picture research by Rebecca Sodergren
Printed and bound in China (CTPS/13)

Acknowledgements
The publishers would like to thank Rosie Green, Howard Horsfall, Clive Bell and Anneli McLachlan.
The author would like to thank Dave Ford, Jan Stephenson and all the team in the Education Development Service of Durham LA, Sarah Sharpe and Sarah Brough.

The publishers and editors would like to thank Deborah Manning, Isabelle Retailleau, Colette Thompson and Andy Garrett at Footstep Productions Ltd, Arthur Boulanger, Lisa Bourgeois, Felix Callens, Juliet Dante, Kathinka Lahaut, Mathew Robathan, Tunga-Jerome Şen and Charlotte Six for their invaluable help in the development of this course.

The author and publisher would like to thank the following individuals and organisations for permission to reproduce photographs:

(Key: b-bottom; c-centre; l-left; r-right; t-top)
akg-images Ltd: album 21/c; Alamy Images: dmac 4/d, Per Karlsson BKWine 2 2/cl, Mark Zylber 2/br; Capital Pictures: 21/a; Getty Images: Garry Wade 25/bl; iStockphoto: Mladen Mladenov 16/a, Paul Willows 29/br; Pearson Education Ltd: Jules Selmes 4/c, 4/e, 9/a, 9/d, 26/tr, MindStudio 4/a, 4/b, 9/c, 15/l, 26/cr, Studio 8 / Clark Wiseman 9/b, 15/bl, 26/1, 26/2, 26/3, 26/4; PhotoDisc 2/tr, 7/br; Photolibrary.com: Guy Christian 22/b, Image Source 29/cr, Stockbroker 25/c, White Star / Monica Gumm 13/bl; Rex Features: Humberto Carreno 21/b, Ken McKay 21/f, Stephen Lock 21/e; Shutterstock: 15/cr, Aleksandr Kurganov 16/e, Alex Staroseltsev 15/c, AND Inc. 2/cr, ASO 16/h, Paul Atkinson 22/d, bioraven 15/tc, Blaz Kure 16/d, Sebastien Burel 22/c, eduard ionescu 15/cl, efiplus 16/f, Elena Elisseeva 2/bc, Graham Prentice 16/c, Alexander Kalina 15/tr, Michael Shake 16/g, Phillip Minnis 22/a, Monkey Business Images 21/bl, Orla 15/tl, risteski goce 16/b, Piotr Rzeszutek 11; Still Pictures: Andreas Meichsner / VISUM 13/br

Cover images: Front: Getty Images: Photographers Choice, Workbook Stock; Pearson Education Ltd / Sophie Bluy; Shutterstock: Andrey Khrolenok, Dibrova, Dmitriy Shironosov, Galina Barskaya, Ints Vikmanis, Nguyen Thai

Audio CD pack: Cover images: Front: Shutterstock: Andrey Khrolenok, Ints Vikmanis; Back: Shutterstock: Ints Vikmanis; on-body CD: Shutterstock: Andrey Khrolenok 0r/CD: Ints Vikmanis 0l CD

All other images © Pearson Education

Every effort has been made to contact copyright holders of material reproduced in this book. Any omissions will be rectified in subsequent printings if notice is given to the publishers.

www.pearsonschools.co.uk

✓ Free online support
✓ Useful weblinks
✓ 24 hour online ordering

0845 630 33 33

Part of Pearson

Tableau des contenus

La France

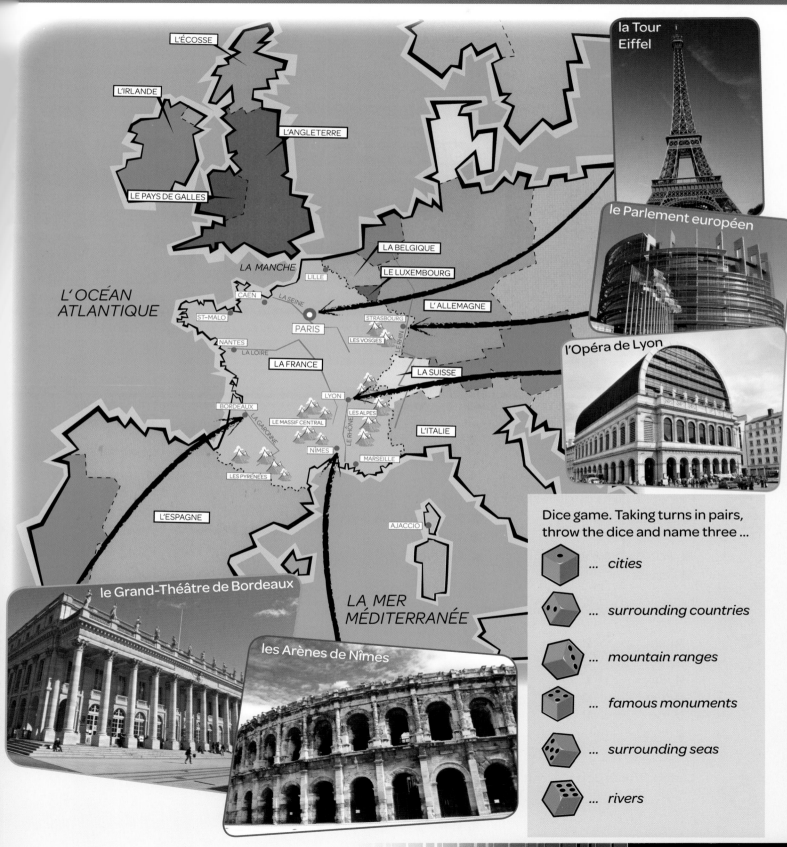

L'ÉCOSSE

L'IRLANDE

L'ANGLETERRE

LE PAYS DE GALLES

LA MANCHE

L'OCÉAN
ATLANTIQUE

LA BELGIQUE

LE LUXEMBOURG

LILLE

CAEN

ST-MALO

LA SEINE

PARIS

L'ALLEMAGNE

STRASBOURG

LE RHIN

LES VOSGES

NANTES

LA LOIRE

LA FRANCE

LA SUISSE

LYON

BORDEAUX

LA GARONNE

LE MASSIF CENTRAL

LES ALPES

L'ITALIE

LE RHÔNE

NÎMES

MARSEILLE

LES PYRÉNÉES

L'ESPAGNE

AJACCIO

LA MER
MÉDITERRANÉE

la Tour Eiffel

le Parlement européen

l'Opéra de Lyon

le Grand-Théâtre de Bordeaux

les Arènes de Nîmes

Dice game. Taking turns in pairs, throw the dice and name three …

… *cities*

… *surrounding countries*

… *mountain ranges*

… *famous monuments*

… *surrounding seas*

… *rivers*

Bonjour!

○ Meeting and greeting people
○ Spelling in French

1 **What are they called? Listen. Who is speaking? (1-5)**

Example: **1** d

> Bonjour!
> Je m'appelle
> Lucas. Au revoir.

> Salut!
> Je m'appelle
> Margot. À plus.

> Salut!
> Je m'appelle
> Thomas. À plus.

> Bonjour!
> Je m'appelle
> Nadia. Au revoir.

> Bonjour!
> Je m'appelle
> Laurent. Au revoir.

a

b

c

d

e

> **!** Notice the **-s** and **-t** are not pronounced at the end of words, e.g. salut, Lucas, Margot, Thomas.

2 **How are they? Listen and draw the correct faces. (1-4)**

  or ?

> Ça va?

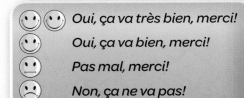

> 😊😊 Oui, ça va très bien, merci!
> 😊 Oui, ça va bien, merci!
> 😐 Pas mal, merci!
> 🙁 Non, ça ne va pas!

3 **Pairwork. Make up dialogues.**

● Bonjour! Comment t'appelles-tu?

■ Je m'appelle <u>Anna</u>.

● Ça va?

■ <u>Oui, ça va bien, merci.</u>

● Au revoir!

■ Au revoir!

Clément: 🙁   Yanis: 😊😊

Anna: 😊   Julie: 😐

4 **Listen and sing the alphabet song.**

A	ah	B	bay	C	say	D	day	E	ugh!
F	eff	G	zhey	H	ash	I	ee	J	zhee
K	ka	L	el	M	em	N	en	O	oh
P	pay	Q	koo	R	err	S	ess	T	tay
U	oo	V	vay	W	doo bl vay	X	iks	Y	ee-grec
Z	zed								

Je connais mon alphabet

Maintenant chantez avec moi

5 **Listen. Which pop star is it? (1-6)**

> Ça s'écrit comment?

> Ça s'écrit ...

Write the phrases out correctly. What is it in English?

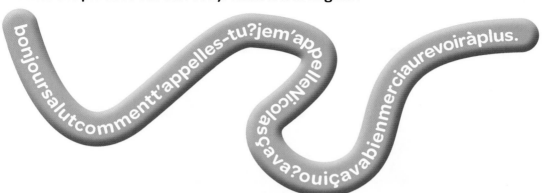

bonjoursalutcommentt'appelles-tu?jem'appellenicolasçava?ouiçavabienmerciaurevoiràplus.

Fill in the gaps with the words from the cloud.

● *Bonjour! (1)_____ t'appelles-tu?*

■ *Je (2) _____ Michael.*

● *Ça (3) _____ comment?*

■ *M -I -C -H -A -E -L.*

● *Ça va?*

■ *Oui, ça va (4) _____ , merci.*

● *Au revoir!*

■ *Au (5)_____ !*

bien

s'écrit   revoir

m'appelle

comment

Put the sentences into the correct order.

1 Et ça s'écrit comment?

4 À plus, Olivia!

7 À plus!

2 O-L-I-V-I-A.

5 Je m'appelle Olivia.

8 Salut! Comment t'appelles-tu?

3 Salut!

6 Ça va?

9 Non, ça ne va pas.

Create a comic strip of two people meeting and greeting each other.

• Put the French in speech bubbles.

• Ensure that you can see it is happening in France or a French speaking country!

Bonjour, comment t'appelles-tu?

Bonjour. Je m'appelle Amina.

...

...

Quel âge as-tu?

- Counting to 21
- Saying how old you are

Listen and repeat.

1	2	3		10	11	12	13
un	deux	trois		dix	onze	douze	treize
4	5	6		14	15	16	17
quatre	cinq	six		quatorze	quinze	seize	dix-sept
7	8	9		18	19	20	21
sept	huit	neuf		dix-huit	dix-neuf	vingt	vingt-et-un

Listen. Which number is it? (1-10)

Example: **1** 14

In groups. Brain teaser.

- Work in groups of four. Count up to 21 in French, each person saying a number and working round the group.
- Replace multiples of **3** with **wizz** and multiples of **7** with **bopp**. **21** is **wizz-bopp**. How quickly can you do it without making a mistake?

Lotto. Who wins? Find the winning card.

Nicolas

3	5	7	12	13	16

Camille

3	5	10	12	17	20

Maxime

3	5	8	12	17	18

Romane

3	6	8	13	17	18

Listen. Who is it? (1-6)

Example: **1** Claire

Quel âge as-tu?

J'ai ... ans.

Practise these words – it feels as if the **-n** *is in your nose! Try pinching your nose when you say them!*

un	**vingt**	**Quentin**
cinq	**Manon**	**Tristan**
quinze	**onze**	**ans**

Hugo

Claire

Tristan

Clémence

Manon

Quentin

Finish the sums in French.

1 deux + trois = _____
2 quatre × trois = _____
3 dix-neuf − quinze = _____
4 vingt ÷ quatre = _____

5 neuf + six = _____
6 vingt − quatre = _____
7 seize ÷ deux = _____
8 trois × sept = _____

+	***plus***
−	***moins***
×	***multiplié par***
÷	***divisé par***
=	***égal/ça fait***

What is missing?

1 deux, quatre, _____, huit, _____, douze.
2 vingt, dix-sept, quatorze, _____, _____, cinq.
3 cinq, _____, quinze, vingt, _____.
4 un, trois, _____, dix, quinze, _____.

Read the thread in the chatroom and fill in the table.

SOS Devoirs

 Jer901 Bonjour! Je m'appelle Jérémy. J'ai douze ans. Ça va bien, aujourd'hui. Et toi? Au revoir.

 Melly1998 Salut! Je m'appelle Mélissa. J'ai treize ans. Ça ne va pas, aujourd'hui. À plus.

 **AlexParis93** Bonjour! Je m'appelle Alexandre. Comment t'appelles-tu? Moi, j'ai onze ans. Ça va très bien, aujourd'hui. Et toi? Au revoir.

 Manon35 Salut! Ça va? J'ai quatorze ans et je m'appelle Manon. Aujourd'hui, ça va super bien. Et toi? Salut!

aujourd'hui = today	
Et toi? = And you?	

Name	Age	How are they?
Jérémy	12	. . .

 Write a reply to one of the posts, giving your details.

Put the months in the correct order. Listen. Did you get it right? Listen again and repeat.

a novembre	**d mars**	**g juillet**	**j avril**
b octobre	**e décembre**	**h mai**	**k juin**
c janvier	**f septembre**	**i février**	**l août**

Look at 'é'! The line above the 'e' (acute accent) tells you to pronounce it like 'ay'.

février d**é**cembre Am**é**lie Fr**é**d**é**ric L**é**a R**é**mi Cl**é**ment

---

Pairwork. How would you say the following missing numbers?

20 _____
21 vingt-et-un
22 vingt-deux

23 vingt-t_____
24 _____
25 _____

26 _____
27 _____
28 _____

29 vingt-neuf
30 trente
31 _____

Look at the pattern!

22 = vingt-**deux**, **23** = vingt-**trois**

*Watch out! 21 and 31 are different: add '**et**'.*

21 = vingt-**et-un**, **31** = trente-**et-un**

When are their birthdays? Listen and choose the correct calendar. (1–7)

Example: **1** d

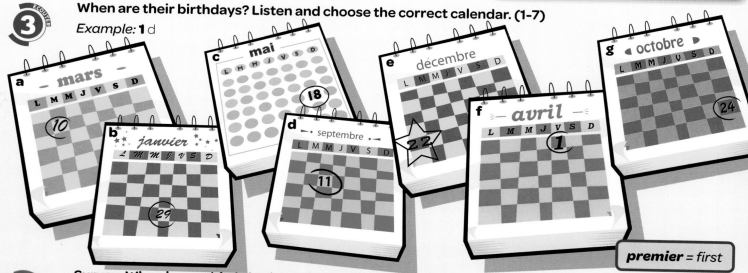

premier = first

Survey: When is your birthday? Ask five people in your class.

Sarah, c'est quand, ton anniversaire?

Mon anniversaire, c'est le vingt-cinq août.

Nom	Anniversaire
Sarah	25 / 08

Listen. Who says the days of the week in the right order: Hélène, Karim, Sébastien or Nathalie?

Did you notice that the months and days in French do not have capital letters?

lundi mardi mercredi jeudi vendredi samedi dimanche

When is their birthday? Write sentences.

Example: Je m'appelle <u>Amélie</u>. Mon anniversaire, c'est le <u>douze avril</u>.

| **Amélie** 12/4 | **Frédéric** 18/3 | **Léa** 2/6 | **Kader** 20/9 | **Rémi** 21/1 | **Simon** 30/10 |

What day is it today? Match the picture with the date.

1 C'est lundi premier septembre.
2 C'est mercredi quatorze février.
3 C'est mardi vingt-six septembre.
4 C'est le dix-huit février.
5 C'est le vingt-cinq décembre.
6 C'est le premier janvier.

a

Joyeux anniversaire!

b

Joyeux Noël!

c

Bonne Saint-Valentin!

d

Bonne année!

e

C'est la rentrée!

f

"¡Hola!" *"Bonjour!"* *"Guten Tag!"*

C'est la fête des langues!

Read the texts. For each person, write down their age and birthday.

a *Bonjour! J'ai douze ans et mon anniversaire, c'est le vingt-huit juillet.*

b *Salut! J'ai onze ans. Mon anniversaire, c'est le trente-et-un octobre. Au revoir.*

c *Bonjour! Mon anniversaire, c'est le dix-neuf mai. J'ai seize ans. Salut!*

d *Salut! J'ai quatorze ans et mon anniversaire, c'est le vingt-deux juin. Et toi?*

Prepare and give a presentation about you or a famous person.

- Say hi and give your name.
- Give your age and birthday.
- Include photos and animations.

Dans mon sac

○ *Saying what there is in your school b*
○ *Using* un, une, des – *the indefinite articles 'a' and 'some'*
○ *Using plurals*

1 **Listen. Which object is it? (1-10)**

Example: **1** d

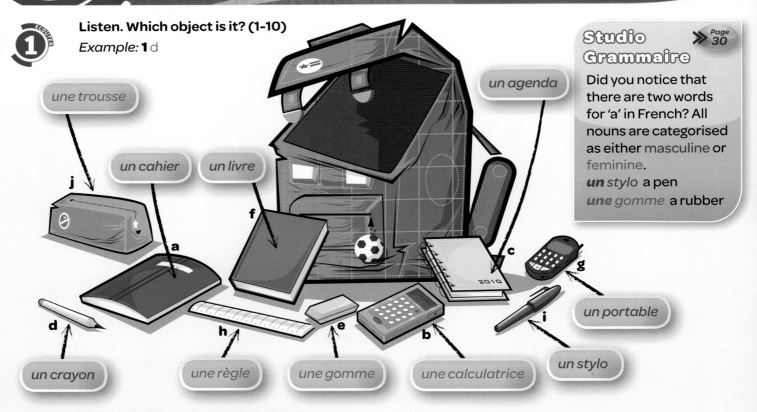

une trousse un cahier un livre un agenda un portable un stylo un crayon une règle une gomme une calculatrice

> **Studio Grammaire** » Page 30
>
> Did you notice that there are two words for 'a' in French? All nouns are categorised as either masculine or feminine.
> **un** *stylo* a pen
> **une** *gomme* a rubber

2 **Pairwork. What am I talking about?**

● *Dans mon sac, il y a un livre.*
■ *C'est ... f!*
● *Bravo ! À toi!*

■ *Dans mon sac, il y a une trousse.*
● *C'est j!*

> **il y a** = *there is*

3 **Listen. Which pencil case is it? (1-4)**

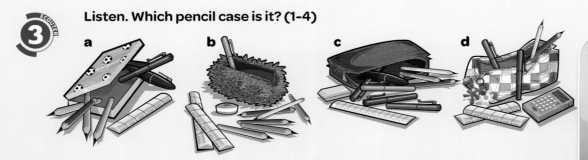

a b c d

> **Studio Grammaire** » Page 30
>
> To make a noun plural add **-s** as in English. Listen again to exercise 3. Did you hear that the **-s** on the end of the word is not pronounced?

4 **Memory game. How many items can you remember?**

● *Dans mon sac, il y a un crayon.*
■ *Dans mon sac, il y a un crayon et deux agendas.*
◆ *Dans mon sac, il y a un crayon, deux agendas et trois ...*

5 **Listen. What is in their bag? Look at the objects in exercise 1. For each person, note down the letters (a-j) of what is in their bag and how many there are of each (1-4).**

Example: **1** Samuel: 1 g (1 portable), 4 f (4 livres)...

1 Samuel   **2** Amina   **3** Émilie   **4** Matthieu

What objects are these? Write them down.

1 agenda 2 crayon 3 gomme

4 otpealrb 5 txrxoxuxsxsxex

 Which is the odd one out, and why?

1	un cahier	un livre	une gomme
2	un stylo	une règle	des cahiers
3	une calculatrice	une trousse	un crayon
4	des crayons	des agendas	un portable

Studio Grammaire  Page 30

The word for 'some' in French is **des**.

Dans mon sac, il y a des livres.
In my bag, there are some books.

 Copy and complete the text in French.

Bonjour! Je m'appelle Luc. Dans mon

il y a [ ] , [ ] [ ] et [ ] .

Dans ma trousse, il y a [ ] , [ ]

et [ ] . Mon sac est cool, non?

 Categorise the objects in exercise 1. What do you have to bring to school, what is recommended, and what is your choice?

Obligatoire	Recommandé	Choix

 All mixed up! Look at pencil case b in exercise 3 and correct the description.

Dans ma trousse, il y a six stylos, deux crayons, une règle, deux calculatrices et une gomme.

Draw the contents of your bag and write a description.

Example: Dans mon sac, il y a ...

1 Listen and write down the objects in the right order. (1-12)

Example: **k**, …

a la chaise
b la fenêtre
c le bureau
d la porte
e le professeur
f la table
g le tableau
h l'ordinateur
i le tableau interactif
j les livres
k la salle de classe
l les élèves

2 Listen. What is in the classroom? Match the numbers and the objects.

a   b   c   d   e   f

20   10   18   2   8   6

3 Pairwork. What is in your classroom? Show your partner round the room.

● *Voilà le bureau!*

■ *Voilà le professeur Monsieur … / Madame … !*

Studio Grammaire 》 Page 30

Did you notice that there are four words for 'the' in French?

le = the (for masculine nouns)

la = the (for feminine nouns)

les = the (for plural nouns)

l' = the (in front of nouns starting with a vowel)

If the noun starts with a vowel, **le** or **la** becomes **l'** as in **l'ordinateur**.

4 Listen to the sounds. What instructions do they correspond to? (1-5)

a Fermez la porte!

c Écoutez le professeur!

e Asseyez-vous!

b Ouvrez la fenêtre!

d Regardez le tableau interactif!

Untangle the word snake. Write out the words in French and English.

Example: le bureau = the desk

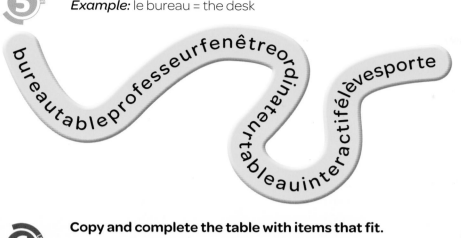

bureautableprofesseurfenêtreordinateurtableauinteractifélèvesporte

Studio Grammaire

It is important to remember accents when writing in French. Three accents can appear on the letter 'e':

é – the acute accent   eg **é**coutez!

è – the grave accent   eg él**è**ves

ê – the circumflex   eg la fen**ê**tre

Copy and complete the table with items that fit.

Ouvrez	Écoutez	Regardez	Fermez

la fenêtre

le professeur

la porte

le tableau

l'ordinateur

les cahiers

le tableau interactif

Crack the code. What do the symbols stand for?

1 V✦ilà la p✦●✳✶e

2 ✦uv●✳e➤ la fenê✶●✳e

3 Éc✦u✶e➤ le p●✳✦fe◎◎eu●✳

4 ●✳egarde➤ le ✶ableau

Describe your classroom. Copy the text and change the details.

Je m'appelle Thomas. Dans ma salle de classe, il y a quinze tables et vingt-huit chaises. Il y a deux portes et neuf fenêtres. Il y a deux bureaux et un tableau interactif. Il y a quatre ordinateurs. Le professeur s'appelle Mme Panesar.

Studio Grammaire » Page 30

Remember that not all words simply add **–s** to make the plural form. Watch out for:

les tableau**x** = the boards

les bureau**x** = the desks

Draw and label a classroom from another country.

- Use one of the pictures or look for your own.
- What is similar to your classroom?
- What is different from your classroom?

il y a = there is

J'adore le judo

- Saying what you like and dislike
- Talking about hobbies

1 Listen. What activities do they like? (1-10)

Example: **1** f

a **le foot**

b **le rugby**

c **le tennis**

d **le vélo**

e **le skate**

f **le judo**

g **les jeux vidéo**

h **la danse**

i **la musique**

j **la gymnastique**

2 Listen. Note down the activity and their opinion. (1-8)

Example: **b**

❤	j'aime	✗	je n'aime pas
❤❤	j'adore	✗✗	je déteste

3 Pairwork. Discuss what activities you enjoy.
- ● *Tu aimes le judo?*
- ■ *Oui, j'adore le judo. Tu aimes le skate?*
- ● *Non, je déteste le skate. Tu … ?*

4 Listen and make notes. What do they like and dislike? What other details are mentioned? (1-4)

c'est	it's	nul	rubbish
super	great	ennuyeux	boring
intéressant	interesting	je préfère	I prefer

5 Follow the lines and write a sentence which corresponds to the pictures.

Example: **1** J'adore le rugby.

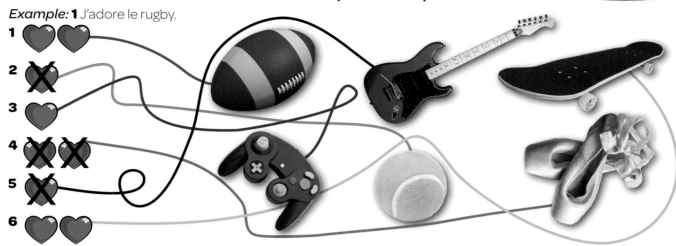

1 ♥♥
2 ✗
3 ♥
4 ✗✗
5 ✗♥
6 ♥♥

6 Read the text and find the following details:

a two positive opinions

b two negative opinions

c how to say 'and' and how to say 'but'

d what Anthony's favourite activity is

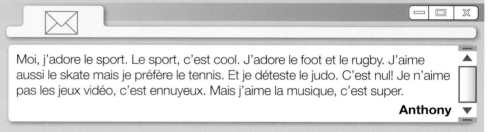

Moi, j'adore le sport. Le sport, c'est cool. J'adore le foot et le rugby. J'aime aussi le skate mais je préfère le tennis. Et je déteste le judo. C'est nul! Je n'aime pas les jeux vidéo, c'est ennuyeux. Mais j'aime la musique, c'est super.

Anthony

7 Brain teaser. Note what Sarah and Lucas think of various activities and, using the graph, decide when each activity took place.

Sarah

Salut! J'adore les jeux vidéo, c'est cool, mais je déteste la musique. J'adore le foot mais je déteste le tennis. C'est nul.
Et je n'aime pas le judo. J'aime le skate, et j'aime aussi le vélo.

Lucas

Bonjour! Moi, j'adore le football. C'est mon sport préféré. J'adore aussi le tennis. Je suis très sportif. J'aime aussi le judo, mais je déteste le skate et la musique. Je n'aime pas le vélo et je n'aime pas les jeux vidéo.

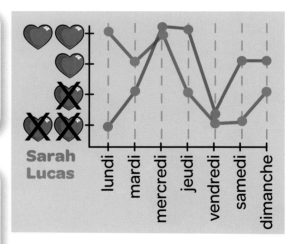

8 Prepare and give a presentation about what you like and don't like.

How many of the statements can you manage? Challenge yourself!

Say what you love and like	✔
Say what you dislike and hate	
Say what you prefer using *je préfère*	
Give two reasons using *c'est …*	
Include *et* (and) and *mais* (but)	

○ Saying what colours things are
○ Using adjectives

1 Listen. Which colour is it? (1-10)

Example: **1** c

a	blanc	**f**	rose
b	jaune	**g**	bleu
c	orange	**h**	vert
d	marron	**i**	gris
e	rouge	**j**	noir

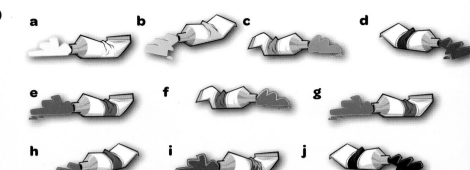

a b c d

e f g

h i j

2 In groups of three. Which colours am I thinking of?

- Player 1 secretly writes down two colours in French.
- Players 2 and 3 take turns in guessing which two colours have been chosen.
- Concentrate! Player 1 can only give the number of colours that are correct: *zéro, un* or *deux.*

● *Rose et orange?*
■ *Zéro!*
▲ *Bleu et rose?*
■ *Un!*
● *Rose et vert?*
■ *Un!*
▲ *Vert et bleu?*
■ *Deux! Bravo!*

vert
bleu

3 Listen. Which scooter is it? Which car is it? (1-6)

Example: **1** d

a b c d e f g h

4 Pairwork. Which scooter do you prefer? Which car do you prefer?

Example:

● *Tu préfères quel scooter?*
■ *Je préfère le scooter orange.*

● *Tu préfères quelle voiture?*
■ *Je préfère la voiture verte.*

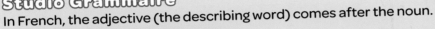

Studio Grammaire

 Page 31

In French, the adjective (the describing word) comes after the noun.

le scooter **bleu**   the **blue** scooter

la voiture **rouge** the **red** car

Look! An extra **-e** is added to some of the colours when the noun is feminine.

Listen! It may make them sound different too!

le scooter / bleu / vert / jaune / rouge

la voiture / bleu**e** / vert**e** / jaune / rouge

Find the odd one out.

1 jaune **bleu** vert noir

2 gris rose rouge **noir**

3 rose vert **jaune** gris

4 **marron** orange gris bleu

5 bleu rouge vert marron

6 jaune gris **marron** blanc

What colour does that make?

Example:

1 rouge + jaune = orange

Write the colour adjectives in the right place in the diagram below.

le scooter blanc bleu gris jaune marron noir orange rose rouge vert

la voiture blanche bleue grise jaune marron noire orange rose rouge verte

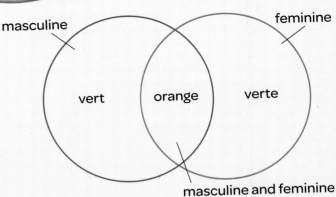

masculine — feminine

vert | orange | verte

masculine and feminine

Look at the photos on page 16. Write an article for your blog.

- Say whether you like each of the cars and scooters in the photos or not.
- Use the key language box to help you – remember to check the endings on the colours.
- You can join some sentences together with *et* (and) and *mais* (but).

✓✓	Je préfère	le scooter	blanc / bleu / gris / jaune / marron / noir / orange / rose / rouge / vert
✓	J'aime		
✗	Je n'aime pas	la voiture	blan**che** / bleu**e** / gris**e** / jaune / marron / noir**e** / orange / rose / rouge / ver**te**
✗✗	Je déteste		

 LIRE
 ÉCRIRE
 LIRE
 ÉCRIRE

1 Listen. Which animal have they got? (1–12)

Example: **1** 5

- **9** un serpent
- **5** un hamster
- **7** un oiseau
- **8** un poisson rouge
- **4** un cochon d'Inde
- **12** Je n'ai pas d'animal.
- **1** un chat
- **2** un cheval
- **10** une souris
- **6** un lapin
- **11** une tortue
- **3** un chien

2 Pairwork brain teaser. Which animal is it? Make sums using the numbers in exercise 1 and find the answers!

- *Un cheval **et** un oiseau? (2+7)*
- ■ *Ça fait un serpent! (= 9)*

```
+   et
−   moins
=   ça fait .../ égal...
```

3 Listen and draw the animals (1–8). Be quick! You only have 20 seconds!

4 Survey: What pets do you have? Ask four friends.

- *Tu as un animal?*
- ■ *Oui. J'ai <u>un chien</u> et <u>deux hamsters</u>.*

Name	Pets
Kylie	un chien et deux hamsters
Adam	un chat gris et ...
Ahmed	...

Can you add in colours too?

Studio Grammaire

≫ Page 30

Remember! If there is more than one animal, add **-s** or **-x** at the end of the noun, but don't pronounce it!

un chat → **deux** chat**s**   un lapin → **des** lapin**s**

un oiseau → **six** oiseau**x**   un cheval → **des** chevau**x**

5 Look at the animals in exercise 1. True or false? Correct the sentences.

Example: **1** Faux, c'est un cheval marron.

1 C'est un cheval bleu.
2 C'est un chien orange.
3 C'est un serpent noir.

4 C'est un chat rouge.
5 C'est une tortue verte.
6 C'est un poisson gris.

7 C'est un oiseau marron.
8 C'est une souris noire.

✔ Vrai
✗ Faux

> *Remember! You may need to add an extra **-e** to the colour describing a feminine noun.*

6 Read the text and answer the questions.

Chez le naturaliste

Bienvenue chez moi! J'ai beaucoup d'animaux à la maison. J'adore les animaux! J'ai trois chiens noirs, quatre chats blancs et huit souris grises. J'aime aussi voyager. J'adore les animaux africains! J'ai un lion orange, deux tigres blancs et noirs, et deux girafes jaunes et noires! Je voudrais un hippopotame, mais ils sont trop gros!

gros = big

1 How many stuffed pets does he have and what colours are they?
2 How many African animals does he have and what colours are they?
3 What animal would he like to have if he had space?

7 Dictionary work. Translate the sentences.

1 I have a monkey.
2 I have a hen.
3 I have an elephant.

4 I have a blue parrot.
5 I have two green ostriches.

> This is what you find if you look up a word in a bilingual French dictionary.
> ***n*** stands for **noun**
> ***m*** stands for **masculine**
> ***f*** stands for **feminine**
> 'I have a zebra' → *J'ai un zèbre.*

cow nf *vache*
elephant nm *éléphant*
giraffe nf *girafe*
hen nf *poule*
lion nm *lion*
monkey nm *singe*
ostrich nf *autruche*
parrot nm *perroquet*
pig nm *cochon*
sheep nm *mouton*
zebra nm *zèbre*

8 At the farm. Use a dictionary and describe your farm.

- Make sure you find out whether the words are male or female.
- Can you add colours? Check how to spell the colours (page 16).
- Can you add any information about yourself as the farmer? Use your imagination!

Example: Je m'appelle Fernand Fermier et dans ma ferme, j'ai un chien noir, deux moutons blancs et deux …

Ma grand-mère est une hippie!

- Talking about your family
- Using mon, ma and mes

1 Look at Tristan's family and listen. What are they called? (1-10)

Example: **1** Dominique

2 In pairs. Who am I?

- ● *Je m'appelle <u>Dominique</u>.*
- ■ *Tu es <u>mon oncle</u>!*

Tu es = You are

Mon grand-père
Léon

Ma grand-mère
Chantal

3 Look at Tristan's family tree again and listen. Who are they? (1-6)

Example: **1** Corinne

Mon père
Alain

Ma mère
Corinne

Mon oncle
Dominique

Ma tante
Nadia

4 Listen. How old are they?

1 Thomas:_____ ans
2 Tristan: _____ans
3 Noémie:_____ ans
4 Brice: _____ ans
5 Adèle: _____ ans

Mon frère
Thomas

Moi
Tristan

Ma sœur
Noémie

Mon cousin
Brice

Ma cousine
Adèle

5 Listen and repeat.

Ad**è**le
m**è**re
p**è**re
fr**è**re
grand-m**è**re
grand-p**è**re

*Not sure how to pronounce **è**? Easy! Open your mouth, smile and think of the 'e' in 'pet'. Not sure how to write the grave accent? Draw it from the top left to the bottom right.*

6 Which famous family is it? Match the sentences (1–6) to the pictures (a–f).

1 Mon père s'appelle Charles et ma belle-mère s'appelle Camilla.
2 Mes tantes s'appellent Patty et Selma.
3 Mes sœurs s'appellent Aimee et Kelly et ma mère s'appelle Sharon.
4 J'ai deux frères qui s'appellent Romeo et Cruz.
5 J'ai six frères!
6 J'ai deux demi-sœurs et une belle-mère.

> **!** Can you work out what **demi** and **belle** mean? Use the exercise to help you!

7 You are Adèle or Thomas. Describe your family. Write five sentences.

8 Brain teaser. Use the clues to complete the table.

a Je m'appelle Anton et mon père s'appelle Isaac.
b Mon père s'appelle Éric et je m'appelle Lucas.
c Je suis Suzanne et ma mère s'appelle Hélène.
d Je m'appelle Anton, j'ai douze ans et ma mère s'appelle Patricia.
e J'ai onze ans et mon père s'appelle Nassim.
f Mes parents s'appellent Hélène et Samir.
g Je suis Lucas et j'ai treize ans.
h J'ai treize ans et ma mère s'appelle Laure.
i Mes parents s'appellent Colette et Nassim.

Nom	Âge	Mère	Père
Mathis			
Anton			
Suzanne			
Lucas			

11	12	13	14	Colette
Laure	Hélène	Patricia		Nassim
	Éric	Samir	Isaac	

9 Prepare and give a presentation about a family. You can use the photo below or use a photo of your own family.

- Give the names and ages of the family members.
- Join some sentences together with *et* (and) or *mais* (but).
- Can you add in extra information from other units (pets or birthdays for example)?
- At the end, check you used *mon, ma* and *mes* correctly!

Studio Grammaire
There are three words which mean 'my'.

Singular Masculine	Singular Feminine	Plural
mon père my father	*ma* mère my mother	*mes* frères my brothers

(Ma sœur) s'appelle … — (My sister) is called …
(Mes frères) s'appell**ent** … — (My brothers) **are** called …

(Mon père) a 35 ans. — (My father) is 35.
(Mes parents) **ont** 40 ans. — (My parents) **are** 40.

10

J'habite dans un château!

- Saying where you live
- Using *petit* and *grand*

1 Listen. Match the description to the photo. (1–4)

J'habite à Papeete dans une maison.

J'habite dans un appartement à Paris.

J'habite dans une ferme.

J'habite dans un château.

2 Listen. What numbers were thrown? (1–6)

Example **1** 🎲 3, 🎲 3

Où habites-tu? J'habite ...

 dans une petite maison

 dans une grande maison

 dans un petit appartement

 dans un grand appartement

 dans une ferme

 dans un château

  à la campagne

  à la montagne

 au bord de la mer

 dans un village

  dans une ville

 dans la forêt

3 Group work. Guess the dice.
- Secretly, throw the dice twice.
- Say where you live according to the pictures.
- The rest of the group note the numbers.
- They read the numbers. Are they correct?
- Change player.

Studio Grammaire » Page 31

Notice that the words *grand* and *petit* add *–e* as usual but they appear before the noun, not afterwards.

un **grand** village — a **big** village
une **petite** ville — a **small** town

4 Listen. Big or small? (1–5)

5 Pairwork. Ask four people where they live and note the answers.
- ● Où habites-tu?
- ■ J'habite à <u>Hull</u>. J'habite <u>dans une grande ville</u>, <u>au bord de la mer</u>, dans une ...

You throw these dice. Write out where you live.

Example **1** *J'habite dans une grande maison à la montagne.*

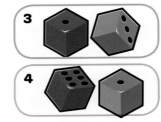

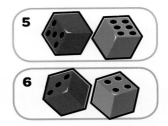

Pairwork brain teaser.

- Choose one of the alternatives from each cloud and note them down.
- Take turns in reading the text from the beginning, guessing your partner's choices.
- Each time you get it wrong, your partner says *'faux'* and it is his or her turn to guess your answers.
- Each time you get it wrong, you have to start at the beginning.

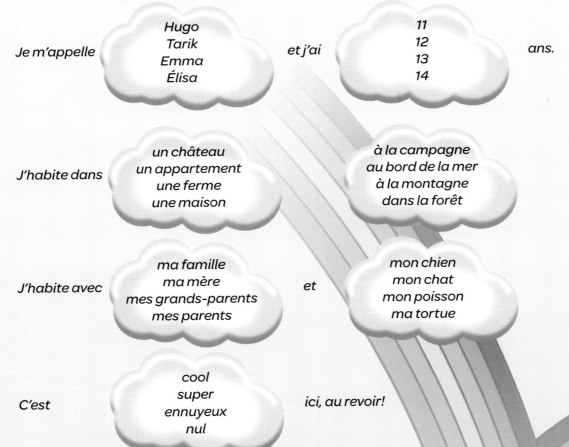

Je m'appelle — Hugo / Tarik / Emma / Élisa — *et j'ai* — 11 / 12 / 13 / 14 — *ans.*

J'habite dans — un château / un appartement / une ferme / une maison — à la campagne / au bord de la mer / à la montagne / dans la forêt

J'habite avec — ma famille / ma mère / mes grands-parents / mes parents — *et* — mon chien / mon chat / mon poisson / ma tortue

C'est — cool / super / ennuyeux / nul — *ici, au revoir!*

**Write a short text about where you live
(use the phrases in exercise 7 to help you!).**

**Imagine you could live anywhere in the world. Where would you live?
Create a presentation about where you live. Add photos!**

11 À table!

Saying what you eat and drink
Ordering in a café

1 Match up the French with the pictures. Listen. Did you guess correctly?

Pour le petit déjeuner ...

je mange ...

je bois...

un thé
un chocolat chaud
un jus d'orange
une tartine
des fruits
un croissant
un pain au chocolat

Pour le déjeuner ...

un café
un sandwich au fromage
une glace
un coca
une pizza
une limonade
un sandwich au jambon

2 Listen. What do they have for breakfast? (1-2)
What do they have for lunch? (3-4)

3 Pairwork. Ask your partner what they have for breakfast and lunch.

● *Qu'est-ce que tu manges pour le petit déjeuner?*
■ *Je mange <u>une tartine</u>.*
● *Qu'est-ce que tu bois pour <u>le déjeuner</u>?*
■ *Je bois <u>une limonade</u>.*

4 Listen. What do they order and how much does it cost? (1-4)

● *Le serveur: Bonjour! Vous désirez?*
■ *Le client: <u>Une pizza et un thé</u>, s'il vous plait.*
● *Le serveur: Ça fait <u>quatre</u> euros. Merci.*

Studio Grammaire ≫ Page 30
a → **un** (masculine), **une** (feminine)
some → **des**

Café français

3€   1€
4€   2€
5€

5 Brain teaser. You spend 6 euros in the *Café français*. How many different combinations of orders are there?

 6 Unscramble the items of food and drink.

1 **azizp**
2 **nttraie**
3 **anmiloed**
4 **alcge**
5 **asircsotn**
6 **lotoccah dhacu**

 7 Read the emails. Who eats what for breakfast?

Example: **a** Idris

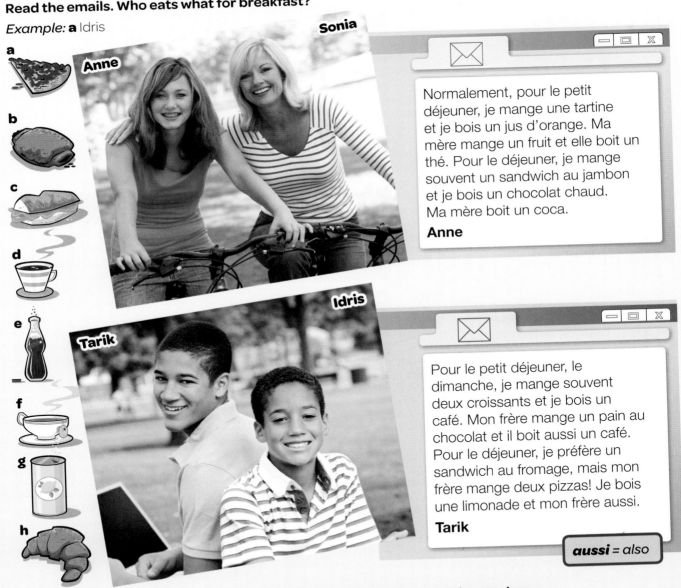

a

b

c

d

e

f

g

h

Normalement, pour le petit déjeuner, je mange une tartine et je bois un jus d'orange. Ma mère mange un fruit et elle boit un thé. Pour le déjeuner, je mange souvent un sandwich au jambon et je bois un chocolat chaud. Ma mère boit un coca.

Anne

Pour le petit déjeuner, le dimanche, je mange souvent deux croissants et je bois un café. Mon frère mange un pain au chocolat et il boit aussi un café. Pour le déjeuner, je préfère un sandwich au fromage, mais mon frère mange deux pizzas! Je bois une limonade et mon frère aussi.

Tarik

aussi = also

 8 Write a short text about what you have for breakfast and for lunch in your home.
Use the texts from exercise 7 as a model.

How many of the following can you include?

Connectives (see unit 6)	✓
Opinions (see unit 6)	
Foods you have looked up in a dictionary (see unit 8)	

● Talking about nationalities and countries
● Using the verb être (to be)

1 Match up the country with the nationality. Listen. Did you guess correctly? (1-6)

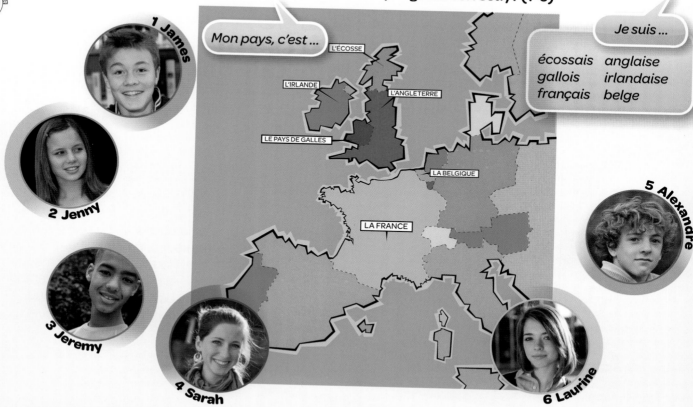

Mon pays, c'est ...

L'ÉCOSSE
L'IRLANDE
L'ANGLETERRE
LE PAYS DE GALLES
LA BELGIQUE
LA FRANCE

Je suis ...

écossais	anglaise
gallois	irlandaise
français	belge

1 James
2 Jenny
3 Jeremy
4 Sarah
5 Alexandre
6 Laurine

2 Listen. Which word do you hear? Is it the male or female form? (1-5)

1 **a** anglais   **b** anglaise
2 **a** écossaise **b** écossais
3 **a** française   **b** français
4 **a** gallois   **b** galloise
5 **a** irlandais   **b** irlandaise

A cedilla is a hook under the letter 'c'. It reminds you that the letter **ç** is pronounced like an 's'. For example: fran**ç**ais.

3 Pairwork. Roll the dice.

● Je m'appelle Jenny et je suis anglaise. Mon pays, c'est l'Angleterre.

■ Je m'appelle Alexandre et je suis français. Mon pays, c'est la France.

Studio Grammaire » Page 31
The verb **être** (to be)
Je **suis**   I am
Tu **es**   You are
Il **est**   He is
Elle **est** She is

4 Listen. Copy and fill in the table. (1-4)

Name	Age	Nationality	Other detail
1 Qaseem			
2			
3			

Copy and complete the table. *Où habites-tu?*

	Mon pays, c'est …	 Je suis …	Je suis …	J'habite …
1	l'Angleterre	anglais	anglaise	en Angleterre
2	la France			
3		gallois		
4			irlandaise	
5	la Belgique			
6		écossais		

Read the texts. What information is given in each text by each person?

Example: **1** a, j, h …

Studio Grammaire

There are two words to say 'in':

la France → *J'habite en France.*
(I live in France.)

le pays de Galles → *J'habite au pays de Galles.*
(I live in Wales.)

1 Bonjour! Je m'appelle Lucy et j'habite en Angleterre. J'habite dans une grande maison au bord de la mer avec mon père et ma mère. Mon anniversaire, c'est le trois juin. J'adore la musique pop.

2 Salut! Je m'appelle Théo et j'ai seize ans. Je suis français. Mon pays, c'est la France. J'habite avec mon père et ma sœur dans un appartement. J'ai aussi deux chats. J'adore les animaux.

3 Je m'appelle Clémence et j'habite en Belgique. Mon anniversaire, c'est le huit janvier. J'habite dans une petite maison à la montagne. Je n'aime pas la montagne. Je préfère la ville. J'adore le shopping!

4 Salut! Je suis Angus et je suis écossais. J'ai treize ans et j'adore le sport. J'habite à Glasgow dans un appartement avec ma mère et Rufus, mon chien. Je n'aime pas la danse!

a name
b age
c birthday
d likes
e dislikes
f family details
g pets
h house details
i nationality
j country

Read the texts again. Correct the sentences in French.

1 Lucy est galloise.
2 Elle déteste la musique pop.
3 Théo a treize ans.
4 Théo habite dans une grande maison.
5 Clémence est française.
6 La mère d'Angus s'appelle Rufus.

Studio Grammaire » *Page 31*

habiter	to live
j'habite	I live
tu habites	you live
il habite	he lives
elle habite	she lives

Write a profile of a famous sports personality.

- Use the categories a–j in exercise 6 to research information about your famous sports personality.
- Ready for a challenge? Use the **il** (he) or **elle** (she) form.

○ *Talking about the weather*
○ *Exploring rhyming and syllables*

1 Listen. What is the weather like? Write the correct letter. (1-10)

Quel temps fait-il?

a Il fait chaud.
b Il fait froid.
c Il y a du soleil.
d Il y a du vent.
e Il y a du brouillard.

f Il y a des nuages.
g Il y a de l'orage.
h Il pleut.
i Il neige.
j Il gèle.

2 Look at the map. Listen and decide whether the statements are true or false. (1-6)

LILLE
PARIS
ST-MALO
STRASBOURG
NANTES
LYON
BORDEAUX
NICE
MARSEILLE
BASTIA

3 Pairwork. What is the weather like?

● *Quel temps fait-il à Lyon ?*
■ *À Lyon, il y a des nuages.*

4 Listen and complete the table. What is the weather like in different seasons? (1-4)

	au printemps	en été	en automne	en hiver
1 en Angleterre				
2 au Congo				
3 au Brésil				
4 en Russie				

5 Complete the rap by matching up the endings with the beginnings. They must rhyme!

Quel temps fait-il à Saint-Malo? À Saint-Malo, ...
Quel temps fait-il à Casablanca? À Casablanca, ...
Quel temps fait-il à Liège? À Liège, ...
Quel temps fait-il à Bruxelles? À Bruxelles, ...
Quel temps fait-il à Montbéliard? À Montbéliard, ...
Quel temps fait-il à Milan? À Milan, ...

il y a du vent   il y a du brouillard   il gèle   il neige   il fait chaud   il fait froid

6 Can you write your own rap with different cities?

7 Read the weather forecast and answer the questions.

Quel temps fait-il à Nice, aujourd'hui? À Nice, au bord de la mer, le matin il pleut et il y a des nuages. L'après-midi, il fait froid et il y a du brouillard. Le soir, il gèle. Bizarre! Ce n'est pas normal! Normalement, il y a du soleil ... Il fait souvent très chaud et aussi, le soir, il y a des orages!

1 What is the weather like today?
2 What is the weather normally like?
3 Find three time references.
4 Find two frequency words.

Make your writing more interesting and add more details about time and frequency.

today	aujourd'hui	normally	normalement
in the morning	le matin	often	souvent
in the afternoon	l'après-midi	from time to time	de temps en temps
in the evening	le soir		

8 Prepare a weather forecast for 1st June 2112.

- Are you positive about the future? Do you think the weather will improve?
- Or are you negative about the future? Do you think the climate changes will be dramatic?
- Include: seasons, weathers and time references

Example: Aujourd'hui, c'est mardi premier juin.
À Londres, le matin, il fait ...

Grammaire

Gender and singular/plural

A **noun** is a word which names a thing or a person. In French, all nouns are masculine or feminine. You have to learn the gender when you learn a new word. In a dictionary, you will see (m) or (f) after the noun (n).

masculine nouns	feminine nouns
le chien (the dog)	*la souris* (the mouse)
un livre (a book)	*une règle* (a ruler)

A noun is singular when it refers to only one person or thing, and plural if it refers to more.
- Most nouns in French, as in English, form their plural by adding **-s.**
  le crayon (singular: the pen) → *les crayons* (plural: the pens)
- Words ending in **-eau** add **-x.**
  un bureau (singular: one/a desk) → *deux bureaux* (plural: two desks)
- Words ending in **-al** change and end in **-aux.**
  un animal (singular: one/an animal) → *deux animaux* (plural: two animals)

1 Make these plural.

1	*crayon*	→	*deux*	_____	**5**	*château*	→	*les* _____
2	*cheval*	→	*trois*	_____	**6**	*trousse*	→	*deux* _____
3	*professeur*	→	*quatre*	_____	**7**	*anniversaire*	→	*les* _____
4	*règle*	→	*cinq*	_____	**8**	*gâteau*	→	*dix* _____

Articles

The **definite article** is the word 'the'. There are three words for 'the' in French:

le (masculine) *le stylo* (the pen)
la (feminine) *la trousse* (the pencil case)
les (plural) *les crayons* (the pencils)

Watch out! **Le** and **la** become **l'** before a vowel or *h* e.g. *l'ordinateur* (the computer). You use the definite article before nouns when talking about likes and dislikes e.g. *J'adore **la** musique.*

The **indefinite article** is the word *a* (or *some* in the plural). There are two words for *a* in French:

un (masculine) *un stylo* (a pen)
une (feminine) *une trousse* (a pencil case)
des (plural) *des crayons* (some pencils)

2 Translate these words using the dictionary page below.

1 the dessert
2 a turkey
3 the showers
4 the drawings
5 a dice
6 some dictionaries
7 the tooth
8 the dance

D	*danse* (nf)	dance
	dé (nm)	dice
	dent (nf)	tooth
	dessert (nm)	dessert
	dessin (nm)	drawing
	dictionnaire (nm)	dictionary
	dinde (nf)	turkey
	douche (nf)	shower

Adjectives

Most adjectives come **after the noun** that they are describing.

*un chien **noir***   a black dog

Some short common adjectives come before the noun, e.g. ***grand*** and ***petit.***

*un **petit** chien*   a small dog

3 Unscramble these phrases and translate them into English.

   1 *petit / le / chien*

   2 *maison / une / grande*

   3 *souris / une / blanche*

   4 *village / petit / le*

   5 *crayons / bleus / les*

   6 *la / trousse / petite*

Adjectives change according to whether the noun being described is masculine, feminine, singular or plural (some are irregular, but the following rule applies to most adjectives).

For feminine, add *-e*   *une souris vert**e***   (a green mouse)

For masculine plural, add *-s*   *deux chiens bleu**s***   (two blue dogs)

For feminine plural, add *-es*   *des trousses noir**es***   (some black pencil cases)

4 Choose the correct form of the adjective.

   1 *un chien <u>noire</u> / <u>noirs</u> / <u>noir</u>*

   2 *deux serpents <u>vert</u> / <u>verts</u> / <u>vertes</u>*

   3 *des crayons <u>grise</u> / <u>gris</u> / <u>grises</u>*

   4 *le stylo <u>bleues</u> / <u>bleue</u> / <u>bleu</u>*

   5 *trois <u>grands</u> / <u>grand</u> / <u>grande</u> chats*

   6 *une souris <u>blanc</u> / <u>blanches</u> / <u>blanche</u>*

Mon, ma, mes

The word for *my* changes according to whether the noun possessed is **masculine**, **feminine**, or **plural**.

(masculine)   ***mon** crayon*   my pencil

(feminine)   ***ma** trousse*   my pencil case

(plural)   ***mes** règles*   my rulers

5 Use your answers to exercise 2 and choose the correct word for 'my' for each of the dictionary entries.

Verbs in the present tense

The present tense is used to describe **what is happening now** or **what usually happens**. The endings change depending upon who is doing the action: ***je*** (I), ***tu*** (you), ***il*** (he) or ***elle*** (she). The ***tu*** form always ends in *-s*.

être (to be)	***avoir*** (to have)	***s'appeller*** (to be called)	***habiter*** (to live)	***aimer*** (to like)	***détester*** (to hate)
je suis	*j'ai*	*je m'appelle*	*j'habite*	*j'aime*	*je déteste*
tu es	*tu as*	*tu t'appelles*	*tu habites*	*tu aimes*	*tu détestes*
il est	*il a*	*il s'appelle*	*il habite*	*il aime*	*il déteste*
elle est	*elle a*	*elle s'appelle*	*elle habite*	*elle aime*	*elle déteste*

6 How do you say the following in French?

   1 he is

   2 you have

   3 I live

   4 he is called

   5 she likes

   6 you hate

Language Learning Skills

Learning vocabulary

1 **Look, say, cover, write, check.** Use this strategy when trying to memorise vocabulary.
2 **Sticky notes.** Write new words on sticky notes and stick them around your bedroom or in places where you will see them regularly. When learning vocabulary, 'a little and often' is better than 'a lot only once'.
3 **Language links.** Make links in your mind when you are learning a new word. Is it like English? Does it remind you of another word? If so, make a little link. For example, *poisson* looks like poison, so imagine a poisonous fish.
4 **Vocabulary ranking.** List new vocabulary from the easy ones to the most difficult. Don't spend too much time on the easy words. Start with the difficult ones and spend more time learning those!

Listening strategies

1 **Know the task.** Before you hear the recording, make sure you know exactly what you are listening out for. Read the instructions for the listening exercise very carefully.
2 **Guess the answers in advance.** Always think about the range of possible answers beforehand. What could the answer be?
3 **Relax.** Sometimes, when you concentrate too hard, you panic and it stops you hearing properly. Focus on key words and do not panic if you don't understand absolutely everything.
4 **Note-taking.** Try different ways of taking notes. Do you find it better to make notes in English or French? Are symbols or images better for you than words?

Reading strategies

1 **Cognates.** Look for words that are closely related to the French words. Look out for similarities that will help you work out what individual words mean.
2 **Context.** Use the context to help you work out the meaning of new words. If all of the texts are about the pets people have, and you have already spotted *chien, chat* and *lapin,* when someone else says that they have a *tortue,* you could make an educated guess at tortoise.
3 **References.** Where can you look if you don't know the meaning of a word? Make sure that you know where vocabulary lists are and how to use a simple dictionary!
4 **Structure of text.** The answers to an exercise are usually in the same order as the text. If you have found the answers to number one and number three, the answer to number two will probably be in between.

Study skills

1 **Stay organised.** Keep all of your French work together in a folder. Stick to a system – know where you keep vocabulary, grammar notes and exercises.
2 **Check and redraft.** Always check over your work. Focus on checking particular elements in the text, e.g. spelling and accents, verb endings, etc.
3 **Work with others.** Working with others can be more effective, since you can help each other when you are stuck, and it is more motivating. Get someone at home to help test you!
4 **Review targets.** Don't just set targets and ignore them. Review them regularly. Read your teacher's marking and respond to it. It really will help you improve!